Oboe - Oboe - Hautbois - Oboe

D1618329

Grade - Grad - Niveau - Grado
**2 - 3**

# BOOGIE FOR WINDS

Markus Schenk - Kurt Brunthaler

# How to play - Spielweisen - Façons de jouer - Come suonare

## English

= play it short: don't accent (play as if you were saying 'dat' or 'dap')

= play it short: accent (play as if you were saying 'dát' or 'dáp')

= play it broadly: don't accent (play as if you were saying 'du')

= play it broadly: accent (play as if you were saying 'dú')

= 'legato tongue': (play as if you were saying 'du-dap')

= bound ('legato'): (play as if you were saying 'du-wap')

## Deutsch

= kurz ohne Betonung (spielen als ob man 'dapp' sagt)

= kurz mit Betonung (spielen als ob man 'dápp' sagt)

= breit ohne Betonung (spielen als ob man 'du' sagt)

= breit mit Betonung (spielen als ob man 'dú' sagt)

= abgesetzt ('legato-Zunge'): spielen als ob man 'du-dapp' sagt

= gebunden ('legato'): spielen als ob man 'du-wapp' sagt

## Français

= jouer de façon brève : ne pas accentuer (jouer comme si tu dis 'dap')

= jouer de façon brève : accentuer (jouer comme si tu dis 'dat')

= jouer de façon large : ne pas accentuer (jouer comme si tu dis 'dou')

= jouer de façon large : accentuer (jouer comme si tu dis 'd'où')

= détacher les notes : jouer comme si tu dis 'dou-dat'

= legato, lier les notes : jouer comme si tu dis 'dou-ouap'

## Italiano

= suonare breve: non accentare (suonare come se dicessi 'dapp')

= suonare breve: accentare (suonare come se dicessi 'dápp')

= suonare tenuto: non accentare (suonare come se dicessi 'du')

= suonare tenuto: accentare (suonare come se dicessi 'dú')

= legato sostenuto: (suonare come se dicessi 'du-dapp')

= legato: (suonare come se dicessi 'du-wapp')

# Contents - Inhalt - Sommaire - Contenuto

| | | | |
|---|---|---|---|
| 1 | | Tuning Note A | |
| 2 | | Tuning Note B$\flat$ | |
| 3 | 4 | Best Friend Boogie | 5 |
| 5 | 6 | Blue Note Boogie | 6 |
| 7 | 8 | Breakfast Boogie | 7 |
| 9 | 10 | Cool Boogie | 9 |
| 11 | 12 | Dino Boogie | 10 |
| 13 | 14 | Game Boy Boogie | 11 |
| 15 | 16 | Roller Blades Boogie | 12 |
| 17 | 18 | Skate Board Boogie | 13 |
| 19 | 20 | Weekend Boogie | 14 |
| | | | |
| ☐ | | Demo Tracks | |
| ■ | | Play Along Tracks | |

# BEST FRIEND BOOGIE

# BLUE NOTE BOOGIE

TRACK 5 6

# BREAKFAST BOOGIE

# COOL BOOGIE

© Copyright 1998 by **De Haske** International , P.O. Box 60, CH-6332  Hagendorn, Schweiz/Switzerland.

# DINO BOOGIE

D.S. al Coda

# GAME BOY BOOGIE

# ROLLER BLADES BOOGIE

D.C. al Coda

# SKATE BOARD BOOGIE

# WEEKEND BOOGIE

♩=120

*mf*

**13**

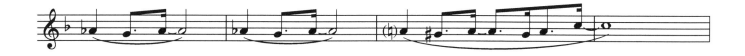

D.C. al Coda

Coda